Graphics and Animation on iOS

Graphics and Animation on iOS

Vandad Nahavandipoor

O'REILLY®

Beijing · Cambridge · Farnham · Köln · Sebastopol · Tokyo

Graphics and Animation on iOS

by Vandad Nahavandipoor

Published by O'Reilly Media, Inc., 1005 Gravenstein Highway North, Sebastopol, CA 95472.

O'Reilly books may be purchased for educational, business, or sales promotional use. Online editions are also available for most titles (*http://my.safaribooksonline.com*). For more information, contact our corporate/institutional sales department: (800) 998-9938 or *corporate@oreilly.com*.

Editor: Andy Oram	**Cover Designer:** Karen Montgomery
Production Editor: Kristen Borg	**Interior Designer:** David Futato
Proofreader: O'Reilly Production Services	**Illustrator:** Robert Romano

Printing History:

May 2011:	First Edition.

ISBN: 978-1-449-30567-3

[LSI]   [2011-05-27]

1305832555

Table of Contents

Preface

Face it—animations make apps really attractive to users. If your app presents a simple user interface, but only does what it says it does, chances are that users will choose a competitor's app, one with a better user interface that makes use of iOS SDK's fantastic animation and graphics capabilities.

This book is written to teach programmers how to incorporate smooth animations, along with skills such as loading custom fonts and drawing images in their apps.

Audience

This book is written for programmers who are fairly new to Cocoa and iOS programming. However, it is assumed that you know basic Objective-C and have done some Cocoa programming. I also assume you know some elementary principles of computer graphics, such as coordinates and the RGB color scheme.

Conventions Used in This Book

The following typographical conventions are used in this book:

Italic

> Indicates new terms, URLs, email addresses, filenames, and file extensions.

`Constant width`

> Used for program listings, as well as within paragraphs to refer to program elements such as variable or function names, databases, data types, environment variables, statements, and keywords.

`Constant width bold`

> Shows commands or other text that should be typed literally by the user.

`Constant width italic`

> Shows text that should be replaced with user-supplied values or by values determined by context.

This icon signifies a tip, suggestion, or general note.

 This icon indicates a warning or caution.

Using Code Examples

This book is here to help you get your job done. In general, you may use the code in this book in your programs and documentation. You do not need to contact us for permission unless you're reproducing a significant portion of the code. For example, writing a program that uses several chunks of code from this book does not require permission. Selling or distributing a CD-ROM of examples from O'Reilly books does require permission. Answering a question by citing this book and quoting example code does not require permission. Incorporating a significant amount of example code from this book into your product's documentation does require permission.

We appreciate, but do not require, attribution. An attribution usually includes the title, author, publisher, and ISBN. For example: "*Graphics and Animation on iOS* by Vandad Nahavandipoor (O'Reilly). Copyright 2011 Vandad Nahavandipoor, 978-1-449-30567-3."

If you feel your use of code examples falls outside fair use or the permission given above, feel free to contact us at *permissions@oreilly.com*.

Safari® Books Online

 Safari Books Online is an on-demand digital library that lets you easily search over 7,500 technology and creative reference books and videos to find the answers you need quickly.

With a subscription, you can read any page and watch any video from our library online. Read books on your cell phone and mobile devices. Access new titles before they are available for print, and get exclusive access to manuscripts in development and post feedback for the authors. Copy and paste code samples, organize your favorites, download chapters, bookmark key sections, create notes, print out pages, and benefit from tons of other time-saving features.

O'Reilly Media has uploaded this book to the Safari Books Online service. To have full digital access to this book and others on similar topics from O'Reilly and other publishers, sign up for free at *http://my.safaribooksonline.com*.

How to Contact Us

Please address comments and questions concerning this book to the publisher:

O'Reilly Media, Inc.
1005 Gravenstein Highway North
Sebastopol, CA 95472
800-998-9938 (in the United States or Canada)
707-829-0515 (international or local)
707-829-0104 (fax)

We have a web page for this book, where we list errata, examples, and any additional information. You can access this page at:

http://www.oreilly.com/catalog/9781449305673

To comment or ask technical questions about this book, send email to:

bookquestions@oreilly.com

For more information about our books, courses, conferences, and news, see our website at *http://www.oreilly.com*.

Find us on Facebook: *http://facebook.com/oreilly*

Follow us on Twitter: *http://twitter.com/oreillymedia*

Watch us on YouTube: *http://www.youtube.com/oreillymedia*

Content Updates

May 27, 2011

- Fixed a minor issue in the text where an *.xib* file was mislabeled as an *.m* file.
- Added a paragraph explaining how readers can add images to their Xcode project, as suggested by a technical reviewer.
- Added the code examples to the O'Reilly catalog page for this book.

Acknowledgments

In 2007, after iOS became so popular among programmers, I started to learn how to program in iOS SDK using an Xcode that was much less advanced than what we use today. My first impression after seeing some iOS apps was: "My God, they look gorgeous!" I had never seen such smooth interfaces, graphics, and animations rendered on a mobile device before, and the big touch-screen added to that excitement. If you are thinking of writing iOS apps that require smooth animations and graphics rendering, then this is the book for you.

Although I did my part to write this book, I feel the need to thank my wonderful colleagues and friends, Andy Oram and Brian Jepson of O'Reilly, for their continuous support and help in every project we have worked on together so far, including the book you are reading right now.

I would also like to thank Sarah Schneider, Rachel James, Betsy Waliszewski, and Gretchen Giles of O'Reilly for always being very helpful and responsive to my annoying requests to create SVN repositories, change book titles, and so on. Thanks also go to Gary McCarville, Kirk Pattinson, Shaun Puckrin, Sushil Shirke, Simon Whitty, Mark Harris, and Shency Revindran for being great friends and colleagues.

A big thanks to you as well for deciding to read this book. I hope that you will enjoy reading this book as much as I enjoyed writing it.

Graphics and Animations

You've certainly seen applications with beautiful graphics effects on iPhones or iPads. And you've probably also encountered impressive animations in games and other apps. When the iOS runtime and Cocoa programming frameworks combine, they make an amazing variety of graphics and animation effects possible with relatively simple coding. The quality of these graphics and animations depends partly, of course, on the aesthetic sensitivities of the programmer and artistic collaborators. But in this short book, you'll see how much you can accomplish with modest programming skills.

I'll dispense with conceptual background, preferring to introduce ideas such as color spaces, transformation, and the graphics context as we go along. I'll just mention a few basics before leaping into code.

In Cocoa Touch, an app is made up of *windows* and *views*. An app with a UI has at least one window that contains, in turn, one or more views. In Cocoa Touch, a window is an instance of `UIWindow`. Usually, an app will open to the main window and the programmer will then add views to the window to represent different parts of the UI: parts such as buttons, labels, images, and custom controls. All these UI-related components are handled and drawn by UIKit.

Some of these things might sound relatively difficult to understand, but I promise you that as we proceed through this book, you will understand them step-by-step with the many examples I will give.

Apple has provided developers with powerful frameworks that handle graphics and animations in iOS and OS X. Some of these frameworks and technologies are:

UIKit
> The high-level framework that allows developers to create views, windows, buttons, and other UI related components. It also incorporates some of the low-level APIs into an easier-to-use high-level API.

Quartz 2D
> The main engine running under the hood to facilitate drawing in iOS; UIKit uses Quartz.

Core Graphics
> A framework that supports the graphics context (more on this later), loading images, drawing images, and so on.

Core Animation
> A framework that, as its name implies, facilitates animations in iOS.

Basic Concepts for Adapting to Different Screen Sizes

When drawing on a screen, one of the most important concepts to grasp is the relation between points and pixels. I'm sure you're familiar with pixels, but what are *points*? They're the device-independent counterpart of pixels. For instance, compare the iPhone 3GS to the iPhone 4. Both devices have 3.5-inch displays. However, the number of pixels that iPhone 3GS can draw in portrait mode is 320×480. The same screen size on the iPhone 4 is capable of drawing twice as many, or 640×960, pixels in portrait mode.

Now imagine you are writing an iPhone app that has only one screen, and that you are simply filling the whole screen with the color green. Imagine that you naïvely specify a rectangular area of 320×480 pixels. When iPhone 3GS users run your app, they will be quite happy because "it does what it says it does"—fill the entire screen with the color green. iPhone 4 users, on the other hand, will be quite unhappy: what they will see is quite different, as shown in Figure 1.

To remedy this problem, Apple introduced device-independent drawing methods to help developers focus on how their shapes and graphics have to appear on a device instead of worrying about the screen sizes and resolutions of different devices that run the same code. To fix the issue we saw in Figure 1, the developer of the app can simply use the relevant APIs to specify the green rectangle in points instead of pixels. That will allow the same code to run on the iPhone 3GS and the iPhone 4, ensuring that the screen on the iPhone 4 will be filled with the rectangle. For this reason, many of the methods that you will see in this book will rely on points (or as Apple calls them, *logical points*) instead of pixels.

 The origin point of the screen on an iOS device is the top-left corner. Screens whose drawing origin is on the top-left corner are also referred to as Upper Left Origin, or ULO, screens. This means that point (0, 0) is the topmost and the leftmost point on the screen, and that positive values of the x axis extend towards the right, while positive values of the y axis extend towards the bottom. In other words, an x position of 20 is further right on the screen than a position of 10 is. On the y axis, point 20 is further down than point 10.

Figure 1. Device-dependent pixel rendering yields different results on different devices

Creating the Project Structure in Xcode

In this book, we will be using view objects of type UIView to draw shapes, strings, and everything else that's visible on the screen.

 I assume you have the latest Xcode from Apple. If not, please head to Xcode's website (*http://developer.apple.com/xcode/*) in order to download it.

In order to be able to incorporate some of these code snippets in an application, I will first show you the required steps to create a new project in Xcode and subclass UIView, where we can place our code:

1. Open Xcode.
2. From the File menu, select New→Project.
3. On the left side of the screen, make sure the iOS category is selected. Select Application under that category (see Figure 2).

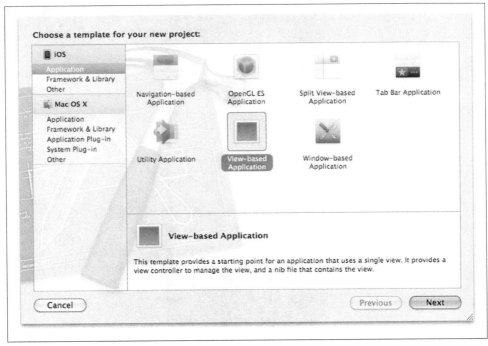

Figure 2. Creating a View-based Application for iOS in Xcode

4. On the right side of the screen, select View-based Application, and press Next (see Figure 2).

5. In the Product Name box (Figure 3), select a name for your project. I've entered *Graphics* and I suggest you enter the same name to avoid confusion later on.

6. In the Company Identifier box, enter a bundle identifier prefix, which will be prepended to the Product Name you chose. This is usually com.company. I have chosen *com.pixolity*.

7. In the Device Family, select iPhone, and then press Next.

8. On the next screen (Figure 4), select where you want to save your project. I've selected Desktop. Press Create.

Now your Xcode project is open. On the left side of Xcode, expand the Graphics group to reveal all the files that Xcode created for us when we created the project. Now we shall create a view object for our view controller. Please follow these steps to do so:

1. Select the Graphics group from the left hand side in Xcode.

2. Right click on the Graphics group and select New File....

3. In the New File dialog box, make sure iOS is selected as the category on the left side, and select Cocoa Touch as the subcategory (see Figure 5).

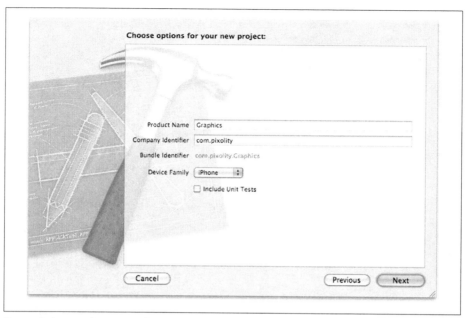

Figure 3. Setting the options for a new project in Xcode

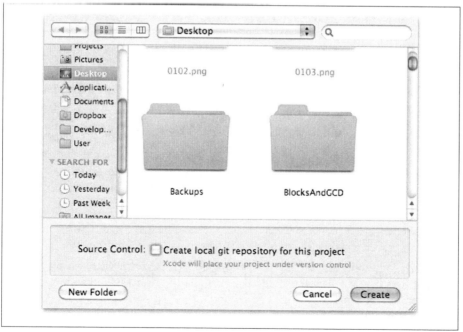

Figure 4. Saving the view-based Xcode project to the desktop

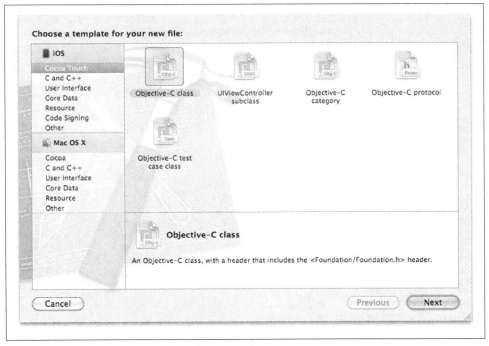

Figure 5. Creating a new Objective-C class in Xcode

4. On the right side, select Objective-C class, and then press Next (see Figure 5).

5. In the next screen (Figure 6), make sure that the Subclass box has *UIView* written inside it, and then press Next.

6. In the Save As dialog, set the file name to *GraphicsViewControllerView.m*.

7. Select Graphics in the Group drop-down box (see Figure 7).

8. Make sure the "Add to targets" checkbox is checked for the project that we created earlier, and then press Save (see Figure 7).

9. On the left side of Xcode's main window, click on the *GraphicsViewController.xib* file. Interface Builder will be displayed on the right side of Xcode's screen, as shown in Figure 8. We will not be using the *.xib* file at this point.

10. From the Xcode menu, select View→Utilities→File Inspector. The file inspector will be displayed, by default, on the right side of Xcode's window.

11. Click somewhere inside the gray view that is created for you in Interface Builder. The contents displayed in File Inspector (on the right) will change to reflect your selection (see Figure 9).

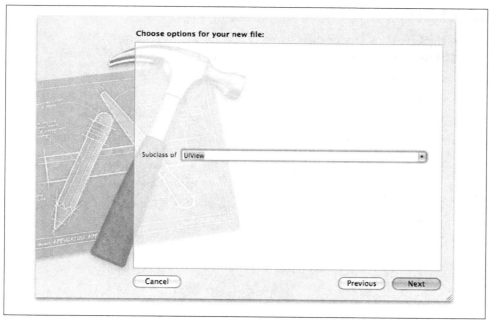

Figure 6. Creating a subclass of UIView

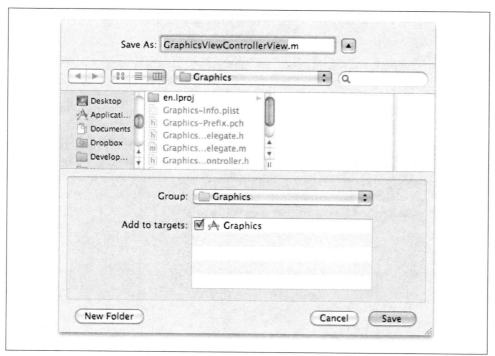

Figure 7. Saving a subclass of UIView

12. In File Inspector, choose the Identity Inspector tab on top (see Figure 10).

13. In the Class box, under the Custom Class section, enter `GraphicsViewController View` (the view object we created before), and press Return on your keyboard.

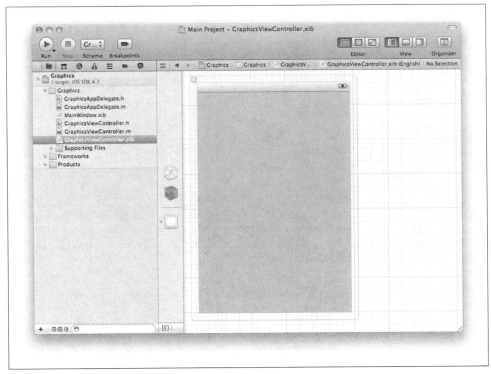

Figure 8. Selecting our view controller's xib file

Now we are ready to start coding. What we did was simply creating a view class of type `UIView` so that later on in this book, we can change the code in that class. Then we used Interface Builder to set our view controller's view class to the same view object that we created. This means that now our view controller's view will be an instance of the `GraphicsViewControllerView` class that we created.

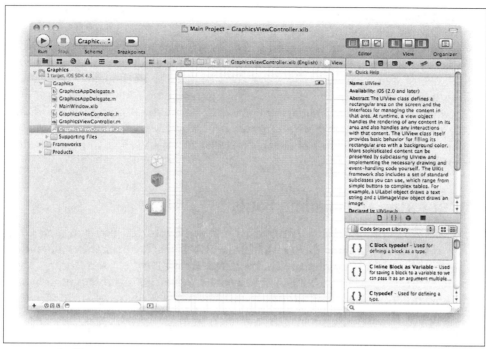

Figure 9. The file inspector in Interface Builder

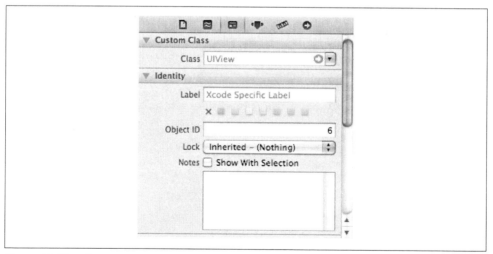

Figure 10. The Identity Inspector, showing our view controller's view object's information

You have probably already looked at the contents of the view object that Xcode generated. One of the most important methods inside this object is drawRect:. Cocoa Touch automatically calls this method whenever it is time to draw the view, and uses it to ask the view object to draw its contents on the graphical context that Cocoa Touch automatically prepares for the view. A graphical context can be thought of as a canvas, offering an enormous number of properties such as pen color, pen thickness, etc. Given the context, you can start *painting* straight away inside the drawRect: method, and Cocoa Touch will make sure that the attributes and properties of the context are applied to your drawings. We will talk about this more later, but now, let's move on to more interesting subjects.

Enumerating and Loading Fonts

Fonts are fundamental to displaying text on a graphical user interface. The UIKit framework provides programmers with high-level APIs that facilitate the enumerating, loading, and use of fonts. Fonts are encapsulated in the UIFont class in Cocoa Touch. Each iOS device comes with built-in system fonts. Fonts are organized into *families*, and each family contains *faces*. For instance, Helvetica is a font family, and Helvetica *Bold* is one of the faces of the Helvetica family. To be able to load a font, you must know the font's face (that is, its name)—and to know the face, you have to know the family. So first, let's enumerate all the font families that are installed on the device, using the familyNames class method of the UIFont class:

```
- (void) enumerateFonts{

  for (NSString *familyName in [UIFont familyNames]){
    NSLog(@"Font Family = %@", familyName);
  }

}
```

Running this program in iOS Simulator, I get results similar to this:

```
...
Font Family = Heiti TC
Font Family = Sinhala Sangam MN
Font Family = Kannada Sangam MN
Font Family = Georgia
Font Family = Heiti J
Font Family = Times New Roman
Font Family = Snell Roundhand
Font Family = Geeza Pro
Font Family = Helvetica Neue
...
```

After getting the font families, we can enumerate the font names inside each family. We'll use the fontNamesForFamilyName: class method of the UIFont class, and get back an array of font names for the family name that we pass as a parameter:

```
- (void) enumerateFonts{

    for (NSString *familyName in [UIFont familyNames]){
      NSLog(@"Font Family = %@", familyName);

      for (NSString *fontName in
           [UIFont fontNamesForFamilyName:familyName]){

        NSLog(@"\t%@", fontName);

      }

    }

}
```

Running this code in iOS Simulator gives me the following results:

```
...
Font Family = Geeza Pro
  GeezaPro
  GeezaPro-Bold
Font Family = Helvetica Neue
  HelveticaNeue-Italic
  HelveticaNeue-Bold
  HelveticaNeue-BoldItalic
  HelveticaNeue
...
```

So as you can see, *Helvetica Neue* is the font family and *HelveticaNeue-Bold* is one of the font names in this family. Now that we know the font name, we can load the fonts into objects of type UIFont using the fontWithName:size: class method of the UIFont class:

```
UIFont *helveticaBold =
  [UIFont fontWithName:@"HelveticaNeue-Bold"
                  size:12.0f];
```

> If the result of the fontWithName:size: class method of the UIFont class is nil, the given font name could not be found. Make sure that the font name you have provided is available in the system by first enumerating all the font families and then all font names available in each family.

You can also use the systemFontOfSize: instance method of the UIFont class (or its bold alternative, boldSystemFontOfSize:) to load local system fonts, whatever they might be, from the device that is running your code. The default system font for iOS devices is Helvetica.

After you have loaded fonts, you can proceed to "Drawing Text" on page 12, where we will use the fonts that we loaded here in order to draw text on a graphical context.

Drawing Text

To draw text, we can use some really handy methods that are built into the NSString class, such as drawAtPoint:withFont:. Before we proceed further, make sure that you have followed the instructions in "Creating the Project Structure in Xcode" on page 3. You should now have a view object, subclassed from UIView, named GraphicsViewControllerView. Open that file. If the drawRect: instance method of the view object is commented out, remove the comments until you have that method in your view object:

```
#import "GraphicsViewControllerView.h"

@implementation GraphicsViewControllerView

- (id)initWithFrame:(CGRect)frame{
  self = [super initWithFrame:frame];
  if (self) {
    // Initialization code
  }
  return self;
}

- (void)drawRect:(CGRect)rect{
  // Drawing code
}

- (void)dealloc{
  [super dealloc];
}

@end
```

The drawRect: method is where we'll do our drawing, as mentioned before. Here, we can start loading our font, and then draw a simple string on the screen at point 40 on the x axis and 180 on the y axis (Figure 11):

```
- (void)drawRect:(CGRect)rect{
  // Drawing code

  UIFont *helveticaBold =
  [UIFont fontWithName:@"HelveticaNeue-Bold"
                   size:40.0f];

  NSString *myString = @"Some String";

  [myString drawAtPoint:CGPointMake(40, 180)
             withFont:helveticaBold];

}
```

In this code, we are simply loading a bold Helvetica font at size 40, and using it to draw the text Some String at point (40, 180).

Figure 11. A random string drawn on the graphical context of a view

In "Constructing, Setting, and Using Colors" on page 13, we will learn how to construct colors and use them to draw colorful texts on our view objects.

Constructing, Setting, and Using Colors

UIKit provides programmers with a high-level abstraction of colors, encapsulated in the UIColor object. This class has a few really handy class methods such as redColor, blueColor, brownColor, and yellowColor. However, if the color you are looking for isn't one of the options provided by such explicitly named UIColor methods, you can always use the colorWithRed:green:blue:alpha: class method of UIColor class to load the color that you are looking for. The return value of this class method is a value of type UIColor. The parameters of this method are:

red
> The amount of red to use in the color. This value can be anything between 0.0f to 1.0f, where 0.0f omits all red and 1.0f makes the red component as dark as possible.

green
> The amount of green to mix with the red in the color. This value also ranges from 0.0f to 1.0f.

blue

> The amount of blue to mix with the red and green in the color. This value also ranges from `0.0f` to `1.0f`.

alpha

> The opaqueness of the color. This value can range from `0.0f` to `1.0f`, with `1.0f` making the color completely opaque and `0.0f` making the color completely transparent (in other words, invisible).

After you have an object of type `UIColor`, you can use its `set` instance method to make the current graphics context use that color for subsequent drawing.

> You can use the `colorWithRed:green:blue:alpha:` class method of the `UIColor` class to load primary colors like red by simply passing `1.0f` as the red parameter, and `0.0f` for the green and blue parameters. The alpha is up to you.

If you look at Figure 11, you will notice that the background color of the view object we have created by default is a really ugly gray color. Let's change that, shall we? Simply find the `viewDidLoad` instance method of your view controller, `GraphicsViewControl ler`, and set the background color of your view to white as shown here:

```
- (void)viewDidLoad{
[super viewDidLoad];
self.view.backgroundColor = [UIColor whiteColor];
}
```

> We will be using instance methods of the `NSString` class to draw text on the current graphics context, as we shall soon discuss.

Now let's load a magenta color into an object of type `UIColor` and then draw the text `I Learn Really Fast` on our view's graphical context using a bold Helvetica font of size 30 (see "Enumerating and Loading Fonts" on page 10 for loading fonts):

```
- (void)drawRect:(CGRect)rect{
// Drawing code

/* Load the color */
UIColor *magentaColor =
  [UIColor colorWithRed:0.5f
                  green:0.0f
                   blue:0.5f
                  alpha:1.0f];

/* Set the color in the graphical context */
[magentaColor set];
```

```
/* Load the font */
UIFont *helveticaBold =
[UIFont fontWithName:@"HelveticaNeue-Bold"
                 size:30.0f];

/* Our string to be drawn */
NSString *myString = @"I Learn Really Fast";

/* Draw the string using the font. The color has
 already been set */
[myString drawAtPoint:CGPointMake(25, 190)
           withFont:helveticaBold];

}
```

The results are shown in Figure 12.

Figure 12. String drawn with a color on a graphical context

We can also use the `drawInRect:withFont:` instance method of the `NSString` class to draw text inside a rectangular space. The text will get stretched to fit into that rectangle. UIKit will even wrap the text if it doesn't fit horizontally within the given rectangle. Rectangular bounds are encapsulated in `CGRect` structures. You can use the `CGRect Make` function to create the bounds of a rectangle. This function takes four parameters:

x

The *x* position of the origin point of the rectangle in relation to the graphics context. In iOS, this is the number of points heading right, starting from the left side of the rectangle.

y

The *y* position of the origin point of the rectangle in relation to the graphics context. In iOS, this is the number of points heading down, starting from the top of the rectangle.

width

The width of the rectangle in points.

height

The height of the rectangle in points.

```objc
- (void)drawRect:(CGRect)rect{
    // Drawing code

    /* Load the color */
    UIColor *magentaColor =
    [UIColor colorWithRed:0.5f
                    green:0.0f
                     blue:0.5f
                    alpha:1.0f];

    /* Set the color in the graphical context */
    [magentaColor set];

    /* Load the font */
    UIFont *helveticaBold =
      [UIFont boldSystemFontOfSize:30];

    /* Our string to be drawn */
    NSString *myString = @"I Learn Really Fast";

    /* Draw the string using the font. The color has
     already been set */
    [myString drawInRect:CGRectMake(100,  /* x */
                                    120,  /* y */
                                    100,  /* width */
                                    200)  /* height */
              withFont:helveticaBold];

}
```

The output is shown in Figure 13.

UIColor is really a UIKit wrapper around the Core Graphics class CGColor. When we get as low-level as Core Graphics, we suddenly gain more control over how we use our color objects, and we can even determine the components from which the color is made. Let's say some other code passed you an object of type UIColor, and you want to detect

Figure 13. Drawing a string in rectangular space

its red, green, blue, and alpha components. To get the components that make up a UIColor object, follow these steps:

1. Use the CGColor instance method of our instance of the UIColor class. This will give us a color object of type CGColorRef, which is a Core Graphics Color Reference object.

2. Use the CGColorGetComponents function to get the components that construct the color object.

3. Use the CGColorGetNumberOfComponents function to determine the number of components that were used to construct the color (red + green + etc.) if need be.

Here is an example:

```
/* Load the color */
UIColor *steelBlueColor =
[UIColor colorWithRed:0.3f
            green:0.4f
             blue:0.6f
            alpha:1.0f];

CGColorRef colorRef = [steelBlueColor CGColor];
```

```
const CGFloat *components =
  CGColorGetComponents(colorRef);

NSUInteger componentsCount =
  CGColorGetNumberOfComponents(colorRef);

NSUInteger counter = 0;
for (counter = 0;
     counter < componentsCount;
     counter++){

  NSLog(@"Component %lu = %.02f",
        (unsigned long)counter + 1,
        components[counter]);

}
```

The output that I get in the console window after running this code is:

```
Component 1 = 0.30
Component 2 = 0.40
Component 3 = 0.60
Component 4 = 1.00
```

Drawing Images

UIKit helps you draw images with ease. All you have to do is to load your images in instances of type UIImage. The UIImage class provides various class and instance methods to load your images. Here are some of the important ones in iOS:

imageNamed: *class method*
> Loads the image (and caches the image if it can load it properly). The parameter to this method is the name of the image in the bundle, such as *Tree Texture.png*.

imageWithData: *class method*
> Loads an image from the data encapsulated in an instance of a NSData object that was passed as the parameter to this method.

initWithContentsOfFile: *instance method (for initialization)*
> Uses the given parameter as the path to an image that has to be loaded and used to initialize the image object.

 This path should be the full path to the image in the app bundle.

initWithData: *instance method (for initialization)*
> Uses the given parameter of type NSData to initialize the image. This data should belong to a valid image.

Please follow these steps to add an image to your Xcode project:

1. Find where the image is located in your computer.

2. Drag and drop the image into Xcode (onto the lefthand side, where the rest of your project files are stored).

3. A new dialog box will appear on the screen. Check the "Copy items into destination group's folder (if needed)" checkbox only if you want the image file to be copied into your project's structure. Uncheck this box if you don't intend to copy the image into your project file, instead allowing Xcode to read it from the original file that you dragged and dropped.

4. In the Folders section, make sure that the "Create groups for any added folders" radio button is selected.

5. In the "Add to targets" section, make sure that you check the targets to which you want to add your image.

 You can search for xcode filetype:png in Google Images to find Xcode's icon as a PNG file. We will be drawing this image on a graphics context to demonstrate how to draw images in this section of the book. I've already found the file and dragged and dropped that image into my iOS app. Now I have an image called *xcode.png* in my app bundle. The image is shown in Figure 14.

Figure 14. Xcode's icon, found by searching in Google

Here is the code for drawing an image:

```
- (void)drawRect:(CGRect)rect{
  // Drawing code

  UIImage *image = [UIImage imageNamed:@"Xcode.png"];

  if (image != nil){
    NSLog(@"Successfully loaded the image.");
  } else {
    NSLog(@"Failed to load the image.");
  }

}
```

If you have the *Xcode.png* image in your app bundle, running this code will print Successfully loaded the image. in the console. If you don't have the image, Failed to load the image. will get printed. For the remainder of this section, I assume you have this image in your app bundle. Feel free to place other images in your app bundle and refer to those images instead of *Xcode.png*, which I will be using in example code.

The two easiest ways to draw an image of type UIImage on a graphics context are:

drawAtPoint: *instance method of* UIImage *class*
    Draws the image at its original size at the given point. Construct the point using the CGPointMake function.

drawInRect: *instance method of* UIImage *class*
    Draws the image in the given rectangular space. To construct this rectangular space, use the CGRectMake function:

```
- (void)drawRect:(CGRect)rect{
  // Drawing code

  /* Assuming the image is in your app bundle
   and we can load it */
  UIImage *xcodeIcon =
    [UIImage imageNamed:@"Xcode.png"];

  [xcodeIcon drawAtPoint:CGPointMake(0.0f,
                                       20.0f)];

  [xcodeIcon drawInRect:CGRectMake(50.0f,
                                     10.0f,
                                     40.0f,
                                     35.0f)];

}
```

The drawAtPoint: call shown above will draw the image at its full size at point (0, 20), and the drawInRect: call will draw the image at point (50, 10) at 40×35 points, as shown in Figure 15.

Figure 15. Drawing an image on a graphics context can be accomplished with two different methods

Aspect ratio is the ratio between the width and the height of an image (or a computer screen). Let's assume you have an image that is 100×100 pixels. If you draw this image at point (0, 0) with a size of (100, 200), you can immediately see on the screen that the image is stretched in height (200 pixels instead of 100). The `drawInRect:` instance method of `UIImage` leaves it up to you how you want to draw your images. In other words, it is *you* who has to specify the *x*, *y*, width, and height of your image as it appears on the screen.

Drawing Lines

When we talk about drawing shapes in iOS or OS X, we are implicitly talking about *paths*. What are paths, you may ask? A path is constructed from one or more series of points drawn on a screen. There is a big difference between paths and lines. A path can contain many lines, but a line cannot contain many paths. Think of paths as series of points—it's as simple as that.

Lines have to be drawn using paths. Specify the start and end points, and then ask Core Graphics to fill that path for you. Core Graphics realizes that you have created a line on that path, and will paint that path for you using the color that you specified (see "Constructing, Setting, and Using Colors" on page 13).

We will be talking about paths more in-depth later (see "Constructing Paths" on page 28), but for now let's focus on using paths to create straight lines. To do this, follow these steps:

1. Choose a color on your graphics context (see "Constructing, Setting, and Using Colors" on page 13).

2. Retrieve the handle to the graphics context, using the UIGraphicsGetCurrent Context function.

3. Set the starting point for your line using the CGContextMoveToPoint procedure.

4. Move your pen on the graphics context using the CGContextAddLineToPoint procedure to specify the ending point of your line.

5. Create the path that you have laid out using the CGContextStrokePath procedure. This procedure will draw the path using the current color that has been set on the graphics context.

Optionally, you can use the CGContextSetLineWidth procedure to set the width of the lines that you are drawing on a given graphics context. The first parameter to this procedure is the graphics context that you are drawing on, and the second parameter is the width of the line, expressed as a floating-point number (CGFloat).

 In iOS, the line width is measured in logical points.

Here is an example:

```
- (void)drawRect:(CGRect)rect{
// Drawing code

/* Set the color that we want
 to use to draw the line */
[[UIColor brownColor] set];

/* Get the current graphics context */
CGContextRef currentContext =
  UIGraphicsGetCurrentContext();

/* Set the width for the line */
CGContextSetLineWidth(currentContext,
                      5.0f);
```

```
    /* Start the line at this point */
    CGContextMoveToPoint(currentContext,
                         50.0f,
                         10.0f);

    /* And end it at this point */
    CGContextAddLineToPoint(currentContext,
                            100.0f,
                            200.0f);

    /* Use the context's current color to draw
     the line */
    CGContextStrokePath(currentContext);

}
```

Running this code in iOS Simulator will show you results similar to those in Figure 16.

Figure 16. Drawing a line on a current graphics context

Let me show you another example. As mentioned earlier, the `CGContextAddLineTo` `Point` procedure specifies the end point of the current line. Now what if we have already drawn a line from point (20, 20) to point (100, 100), and want to draw a line from (100, 100) to (300, 100)? You might think that after drawing the first line, we have to move our pen to point (100, 100) using the `CGContextMoveToPoint` procedure, and then draw the line to point (300, 100) using the CGContextAddLineToPoint procedure. While that will work, there is a more efficient way to do this. After you call the CGContextAddLine ToPoint procedure to specify the ending point of your current line, your pen's position will change to what you pass to this method. In other words, after you issue a method using the pen, it leaves the pen's position at the ending point of whatever it drew. So to draw another line from the current ending point to another point, all you have to do is to call the CGContextAddLineToPoint procedure again with another ending point. Here is an example:

```
- (void)drawRect:(CGRect)rect{
    // Drawing code

    /* Set the color that we want
       to use to draw the line */
    [[UIColor brownColor] set];

    /* Get the current graphics context */
    CGContextRef currentContext =
        UIGraphicsGetCurrentContext();

    /* Set the width for the lines */
    CGContextSetLineWidth(currentContext,
                          5.0f);

    /* Start the line at this point */
    CGContextMoveToPoint(currentContext,
                         20.0f,
                         20.0f);

    /* And end it at this point */
    CGContextAddLineToPoint(currentContext,
                            100.0f,
                            100.0f);

    /* Extend the line to another point */
    CGContextAddLineToPoint(currentContext,
                            300.0f,
                            100.0f);

    /* Use the context's current color to draw
       the lines */
    CGContextStrokePath(currentContext);

}
```

The results are shown in Figure 17. You can see that both lines are successfully drawn without us having to move the pen for the second line.

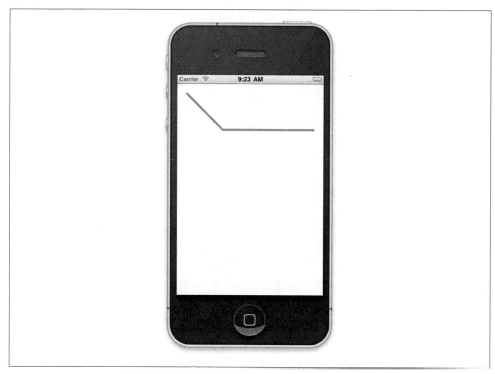

Figure 17. Drawing two lines at once

The point where two lines meet is, not surprisingly, called a join. With Core Graphics, you can specify what type of join you want to have between lines that are connected to each other. To make your choice, you must use the `CGContextSetLineJoin` procedure. It takes two parameters: a graphics context on which you are setting the join type, and the join type itself, which must be of type `CGLineJoin`. `CGLineJoin` is an enumeration of the following values:

`kCGLineJoinMiter`
> Joins will be made out of sharp corners. This is the default join type.

`kCGLineJoinBevel`
> Joins will be squared off on the corner.

`kCGLineJoinRound`
> As the name implies, this makes round joins.

Let's have a look at an example. Let's say we want to write a program that can draw "rooftops" on a graphics context (three of them, one for each join type), and also draws text below each rooftop describing the type of join it is using. Something similar to Figure 18 will be the result.

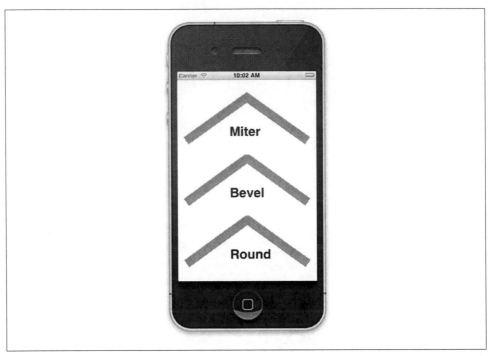

Figure 18. Three types of line joins in Core Graphics

To accomplish this, I've written a method named drawRooftopAtTopPointof:text
ToDisplay:lineJoin:, which takes three parameters:

1. A point at which the top of the rooftop should be placed
2. The text to display inside the rooftop
3. The join type to be used.

The code is as follows:

```
- (void) drawRooftopAtTopPointof:(CGPoint)paramTopPoint
               textToDisplay:(NSString *)paramText
                  lineJoin:(CGLineJoin)paramLineJoin{

  /* Set the color that we want
   to use to draw the line */
  [[UIColor brownColor] set];

  /* Get the current graphics context */
  CGContextRef currentContext =
    UIGraphicsGetCurrentContext();

  /* Set the line join */
  CGContextSetLineJoin(currentContext,
                     paramLineJoin);
```

```
/* Set the width for the lines */
CGContextSetLineWidth(currentContext,
                    20.0f);

/* Start the line at this point */
CGContextMoveToPoint(currentContext,
                    paramTopPoint.x - 140,
                    paramTopPoint.y + 100);

/* And end it at this point */
CGContextAddLineToPoint(currentContext,
                    paramTopPoint.x,
                    paramTopPoint.y);

/* Extend the line to another point to
 make the rooftop */
CGContextAddLineToPoint(currentContext,
                    paramTopPoint.x + 140,
                    paramTopPoint.y + 100);

/* Use the context's current color to draw
 the lines */
CGContextStrokePath(currentContext);

/* Draw the text in the rooftop using
 a black color */
[[UIColor blackColor] set];
/* Now draw the text */
[paramText
 drawAtPoint:CGPointMake(paramTopPoint.x - 40.0f,
                    paramTopPoint.y + 60.0f)
 withFont:[UIFont boldSystemFontOfSize:30.0f]];

}
```

Now let's call this method in the drawRect: instance method of our view object where we have a graphics context:

```
- (void)drawRect:(CGRect)rect{
// Drawing code

[self drawRooftopAtTopPointof:CGPointMake(160.0f, 40.0f)
            textToDisplay:@"Miter"
                lineJoin:kCGLineJoinMiter];

[self drawRooftopAtTopPointof:CGPointMake(160.0f, 180.0f)
            textToDisplay:@"Bevel"
                lineJoin:kCGLineJoinBevel];

[self drawRooftopAtTopPointof:CGPointMake(160.0f, 320.0f)
            textToDisplay:@"Round"
                lineJoin:kCGLineJoinRound];

}
```

Constructing Paths

A series of points placed together can form a shape. A series of shapes put together builds a path. Paths can easily be managed by Core Graphics. In "Drawing Lines" on page 21, we worked indirectly with paths using CGContext functions. But Core Graphics also has functions that work directly with paths, as we shall soon see.

Paths belong to whichever graphics context they are drawn on. Paths do not have boundaries or specific shapes, unlike the shapes we draw on them. But paths do have bounding boxes. Please bear in mind that boundaries are not the same as bounding boxes. Boundaries are limits above which you cannot draw on a canvas, while the bounding box of a path is the smallest rectangle that contains all the shapes, points, and other objects that have been drawn on that specific path. Think of paths as stamps and think of your graphics context as the envelope. Your envelope could be the same every time you mail something to your friend, but what you put on that context (the stamp or the path) can be different.

After you finish drawing on a path, you can then draw that path on the graphics context. Developers familiar with game programming know the concept of *buffers*, which draw their scenes and, at appropriate times, *flush* the images onto the screen. Paths are those buffers. They are like blank canvases that can be drawn on graphics contexts when the time is right.

The first step in directly working with paths is to create them. The method creating the path returns a handle that you use whenever you want to draw something on that path, passing the handle to Core Graphics for reference. After you create the path, you can add different points, lines, and shapes to it and then draw the path. You can either fill the path or paint it with a stroke on a graphics context. Here are the methods you have to work with:

CGPathCreateMutable *function*
> Creates a new mutable path of type CGMutablePathRef and returns its handle. We should dispose of this path once we are done with it, as you will soon see.

CGPathMoveToPoint *procedure*
> Moves the current pen position on the path to the point specified by a parameter of type CGPoint.

CGPathAddLineToPoint *procedure*
> Draws a line segment from the current pen position to the specified position (again, specified by a value of type CGPoint).

CGContextAddPath *procedure*

Adds a given path (specified by a path handle) to a graphics context, ready for drawing.

CGContextDrawPath *procedure*

Draws a given path on the graphics context.

CGPathRelease *procedure*

Releases the memory allocated for a path handle.

CGPathAddRect *procedure*

Adds a rectangle to a path. The rectangle's boundaries are specified by a CGRect structure.

There are three important drawing methods that you can ask the CGContextDrawPath procedure to perform:

kCGPathStroke

Draws a line (stroke) to mark the boundary or edge of the path, using the currently selected stroke color.

kCGPathFill

Fills the area surrounded by the path with the currently selected fill color.

kCGPathFillStroke

Combines stroke and fill. Uses the currently selected fill color to fill the path, and the currently selected stroke color to draw the edge of the path. We'll see an example of this method in the following section.

Let's have a look at an example. We will draw a blue line from the top-left to the bottom-right corner and another from the top-right to the bottom-left corner, to create a gigantic X across the screen.

 For this example, I have removed the status bar from the application in iOS Simulator. If you don't want to bother doing this, please continue to the example code. With a status bar, the output of this code will only be slightly different from the screenshot I'll show. To hide the status bar, find the *Info.plist* file in your Xcode project and add a key to it named UIStatusBarHidden with the value of YES, as shown in Figure 19. This will force your app's status bar to be hidden when it opens.

Key	Type	Value
Localization native development region	String	en
Bundle display name	String	${PRODUCT_NAME}
Executable file	String	${EXECUTABLE_NAME}
Icon file	String	
Bundle identifier	String	com.pixolity.${PRODUCT_NAME:rfc1034identifier}
InfoDictionary version	String	6.0
Bundle name	String	${PRODUCT_NAME}
Bundle OS Type code	String	APPL
Bundle versions string, short	String	1.0
Bundle creator OS Type code	String	????
Bundle version	String	1.0
Application requires iPhone environmen	Boolean	YES
Main nib file base name	String	MainWindow
Status bar is initially hidden	Boolean	YES
Supported interface orientations	Array	(3 items)

Figure 19. Hiding the status bar in an iOS app using the Info.plist file

```objc
- (void)drawRect:(CGRect)rect{
// Drawing code

/* Create the path */
CGMutablePathRef path = CGPathCreateMutable();

/* How big is our screen? We want the X to cover
 the whole screen */
CGRect screenBounds = [[UIScreen mainScreen] bounds];

/* Start from top-left */
CGPathMoveToPoint(path,
                  NULL,
                  screenBounds.origin.x,
                  screenBounds.origin.y);

/* Draw a line from top-left to
 bottom-right of the screen */
CGPathAddLineToPoint(path,
                     NULL,
                     screenBounds.size.width,
                     screenBounds.size.height);

/* Start another line from top-right */
CGPathMoveToPoint(path,
                  NULL,
                  screenBounds.size.width,
                  screenBounds.origin.y);

/* Draw a line from top-right to bottom-left */
CGPathAddLineToPoint(path,
                     NULL,
                     screenBounds.origin.x,
                     screenBounds.size.height);
```

```
/* Get the context that the path has to be
 drawn on */
CGContextRef currentContext =
  UIGraphicsGetCurrentContext();

/* Add the path to the context so we can
 draw it later */
CGContextAddPath(currentContext,
                 path);

/* Set the blue color as the stroke color */
[[UIColor blueColor] setStroke];

/* Draw the path with stroke color */
CGContextDrawPath(currentContext,
                  kCGPathStroke);

/* Finally release the path object */
CGPathRelease(path);

}
```

The NULL parameters getting passed to procedures such as CGPath
MoveToPoint represent possible transformations that can be used when
drawing the shapes and lines on a given path. For information about
transformations, refer to "Displacing Shapes on Graphic Contexts" on page 49, "Scaling Shapes Drawn on Graphic Contexts" on page 52, and "Rotating Shapes Drawn on Graphic Contexts" on page 55.

You can see how easy it is to draw a path on a context. All you really have to remember
is how to create a new mutable path (CGPathCreateMutable), add that path to your
graphics context (CGContextAddPath), and draw it on a graphics context (CGContextDraw
Path). If you run this code, you will get an output similar to that shown in Figure 20.

The next section, "Drawing Rectangles", shows more examples of using paths.

Drawing Rectangles

As we learned in "Constructing Paths" on page 28, you can construct and use paths
quite easily. One of the procedures that you can use on paths in Core Graphics is
CGPathAddRect, which lets you draw rectangles as part of paths. Here is an example:

```
- (void)drawRect:(CGRect)rect{
  // Drawing code

  /* Create the path first. Just the path handle. */
  CGMutablePathRef path = CGPathCreateMutable();
```

Figure 20. Drawing on a graphics context using paths

```
/* Here are our rectangle boundaries */
CGRect rectangle = CGRectMake(10.0f,
                              10.0f,
                              200.0f,
                              300.0f);

/* Add the rectangle to the path */
CGPathAddRect(path,
              NULL,
              rectangle);

/* Get the handle to the current context */
CGContextRef currentContext =
  UIGraphicsGetCurrentContext();

/* Add the path to the context */
CGContextAddPath(currentContext,
                 path);

/* Set the fill color to cornflower blue */
[[UIColor colorWithRed:0.20f
                 green:0.60f
                  blue:0.80f
                 alpha:1.0f] setFill];
```

```
/* Set the stroke color to brown */
[[UIColor brownColor] setStroke];

/* Set the line width (for the stroke) to 5 */
CGContextSetLineWidth(currentContext,
                      5.0f);

/* Stroke and fill the path on the context */
CGContextDrawPath(currentContext,
                  kCGPathFillStroke);

/* Dispose of the path */
CGPathRelease(path);

}
```

Here, we are drawing a rectangle on the path, filling it with cornflower blue, and stroking the edges of the rectangle with brown. Figure 21 shows how the output will look when we run our program.

Figure 21. Drawing a rectangle using paths

If you have multiple rectangles to draw, you can pass an array of CGRect objects to the CGPathAddRects procedure. Here is an example:

```
- (void)drawRect:(CGRect)rect{
  // Drawing code

  /* Create the path first. Just the path handle. */
  CGMutablePathRef path = CGPathCreateMutable();

  /* Here are our first rectangle boundaries */
  CGRect rectangle1 = CGRectMake(10.0f,
                                 10.0f,
                                 200.0f,
                                 300.0f);

  /* And the second rectangle */
  CGRect rectangle2 = CGRectMake(40.0f,
                                 100.0f,
                                 90.0f,
                                 300.0f);

  /* Put both rectangles into an array */
  CGRect rectangles[2] = {
    rectangle1, rectangle2
  };

  /* Add the rectangles to the path */
  CGPathAddRects(path,
                 NULL,
                 (const CGRect *)&rectangles,
                 2);

  /* Get the handle to the current context */
  CGContextRef currentContext =
  UIGraphicsGetCurrentContext();

  /* Add the path to the context */
  CGContextAddPath(currentContext,
                   path);

  /* Set the fill color to cornflower blue */
  [[UIColor colorWithRed:0.20f
                   green:0.60f
                    blue:0.80f
                   alpha:1.0f] setFill];

  /* Set the stroke color to black */
  [[UIColor blackColor] setStroke];

  /* Set the line width (for the stroke) to 5 */
  CGContextSetLineWidth(currentContext,
                        5.0f);
```

```
/* Stroke and fill the path on the context */
CGContextDrawPath(currentContext,
                  kCGPathFillStroke);

/* Dispose of the path */
CGPathRelease(path);

}
```

Figure 22 shows how the output of this code will look when run in iOS Simulator. The parameters that we pass to the `CGPathAddRects` procedure are (in this order):

1. The handle to the path where we will add the rectangles.

2. The transformation, if any, to use on to the rectangles. (For information about transformations, refer to "Displacing Shapes on Graphic Contexts" on page 49, "Scaling Shapes Drawn on Graphic Contexts" on page 52, and "Rotating Shapes Drawn on Graphic Contexts" on page 55.)

3. A reference to the array holding the `CGRect` rectangles.

4. The number of rectangles in the array that we passed in the previous parameter. It is very important that you pass exactly as many rectangles as you have in your array, to avoid unknown behavior by this procedure.

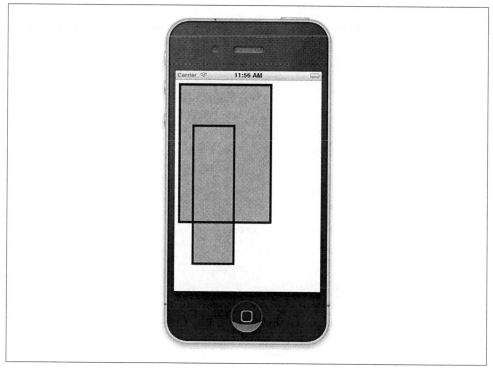

Figure 22. Drawing multiple rectangles at once

Adding Shadows to Shapes

It is easy to draw shadows using Core Graphics. The graphics context is the element that bears the shadow. What that means is that you need to apply the shadow to the context, draw the shapes that need the shadow, and then remove the shadow from the context (or set a new context). We will see an example of this soon.

In Core Graphics, we can use two procedures to apply a shadow to a graphics context:

CGContextSetShadow *procedure*

This procedure, which creates black or gray shadows, accepts three parameters:

- The graphics context on which the shadow has to be applied.
- The offset, specified by a value of type CGSize, from the right and the bottom part of each shape where the shadow has to be applied. The greater the *x* value of this offset is, the farther to the right of each shape the shadow will extend. The greater the *y* value of this offset is, the lower the shadow will extend.
- The blur value that has to be applied to the shadow, specified as a floating point value (CGFloat). Specifying 0.0f will cause the shadow to be a solid shape. The higher this value goes, the more blurred the shadow will get. We will see an example of this soon.

CGContextSetShadowWithColor *procedure*

This procedure accepts the exact same parameters as CGContextSetShadow, with one addition. This fourth parameter, of type CGColorRef, sets the color of the shadow.

At the beginning of this section, I mentioned that the graphics context retains its shadow properties until we explicitly remove the shadow. Let me make that point clearer by showing you an example. Let us go ahead and write code that allows us to draw two rectangles, the first one with a shadow and the second one without a shadow. We will draw the first one in this way:

```
- (void) drawRectAtTopOfScreen{

  /* Get the handle to the current context */
  CGContextRef currentContext =
    UIGraphicsGetCurrentContext();

  CGContextSetShadowWithColor(currentContext,
                              CGSizeMake(10.0f, 10.0f),
                              20.0f,
                              [[UIColor grayColor] CGColor]);

  /* Create the path first. Just the path handle. */
  CGMutablePathRef path = CGPathCreateMutable();

  /* Here are our rectangle boundaries */
  CGRect firstRect = CGRectMake(55.0f,
                                60.0f,
                                150.0f,
                                150.0f);
```

```
/* Add the rectangle to the path */
CGPathAddRect(path,
            NULL,
            firstRect);

/* Add the path to the context */
CGContextAddPath(currentContext,
                path);

/* Set the fill color to cornflower blue */
[[UIColor colorWithRed:0.20f
            green:0.60f
             blue:0.80f
            alpha:1.0f] setFill];

/* Fill the path on the context */
CGContextDrawPath(currentContext,
                kCGPathFill);

/* Dispose of the path */
CGPathRelease(path);

}
```

If we call this method in the drawRect: instance method of our view object, we will see the rectangle drawn on the screen with a nice shadow just like we wanted it, as shown in Figure 23.

Now let's go ahead and draw a second rectangle after the first one. We won't ask for a shadow, but we'll leave the shadow property of the graphics context the way it was for the first rectangle:

```
- (void) drawRectAtBottomOfScreen{

/* Get the handle to the current context */
CGContextRef currentContext =
  UIGraphicsGetCurrentContext();

CGMutablePathRef secondPath = CGPathCreateMutable();

CGRect secondRect = CGRectMake(150.0f,
                            250.0f,
                            100.0f,
                            100.0f);
CGPathAddRect(secondPath,
            NULL,
            secondRect);

CGContextAddPath(currentContext,
                secondPath);

[[UIColor purpleColor] setFill];
```

Figure 23. Shadow applied to a rectangle

```
CGContextDrawPath(currentContext,
                  kCGPathFill);

CGPathRelease(secondPath);

}

- (void)drawRect:(CGRect)rect{
  // Drawing code

  [self drawRectAtTopOfScreen];
  [self drawRectAtBottomOfScreen];

}
```

The drawRect: method first calls the drawRectAtTopOfScreen method, and right after that, calls the drawRectAtBottomOfScreen method. We haven't asked for a shadow for the drawRectAtBottomOfScreen rectangle, yet if you run the app, you will see something similar to what is shown in Figure 24.

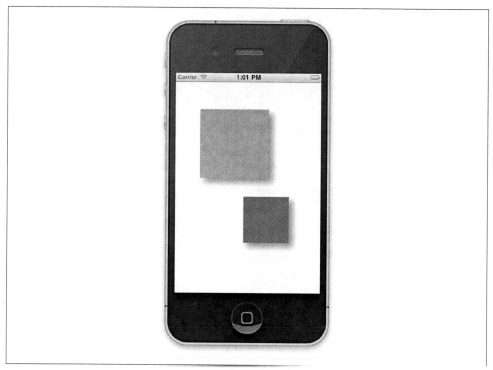

Figure 24. Shadow applied to a second rectangle is not on purpose

It's immediately obvious that the shadow is applied to the second rectangle at the bottom of the screen. To avoid this, we will save the state of the graphics context *before* applying the shadow effect, and then restore the state when we want to remove the shadow effect.

Broadly speaking, saving and restoring the state of a graphics context is not limited to shadows only. Restoring the state of a graphics context restores everything (fill color, font, line thickness, etc.) to the values they had before you set them. So for instance, if you applied fill and stroke colors in the meantime, those colors will be reset.

You can save the state of a graphics context through the `CGContextSaveGState` procedure and restore the previous state through the `CGContextRestoreGState` procedure. So if we modify the `drawRectAtTopOfScreen` procedure by saving the state of the graphics context before applying the shadow, and restore that state after drawing the path, we will have different results, shown in Figure 25:

```
- (void) drawRectAtTopOfScreen{

    /* Get the handle to the current context */
    CGContextRef currentContext =
      UIGraphicsGetCurrentContext();

    CGContextSaveGState(currentContext);

    CGContextSetShadowWithColor(currentContext,
                                CGSizeMake(10.0f, 10.0f),
                                20.0f,
                                [[UIColor grayColor] CGColor]);

    /* Create the path first. Just the path handle. */
    CGMutablePathRef path = CGPathCreateMutable();

    /* Here are our rectangle boundaries */
    CGRect firstRect = CGRectMake(55.0f,
                                  60.0f,
                                  150.0f,
                                  150.0f);

    /* Add the rectangle to the path */
    CGPathAddRect(path,
                  NULL,
                  firstRect);

    /* Add the path to the context */
    CGContextAddPath(currentContext,
                     path);

    /* Set the fill color to cornflower blue */
    [[UIColor colorWithRed:0.20f
                     green:0.60f
                      blue:0.80f
                     alpha:1.0f] setFill];

    /* Fill the path on the context */
    CGContextDrawPath(currentContext,
                      kCGPathFill);

    /* Dispose of the path */
    CGPathRelease(path);

    /* Restore the context to how it was
     when we started */
    CGContextRestoreGState(currentContext);

}
```

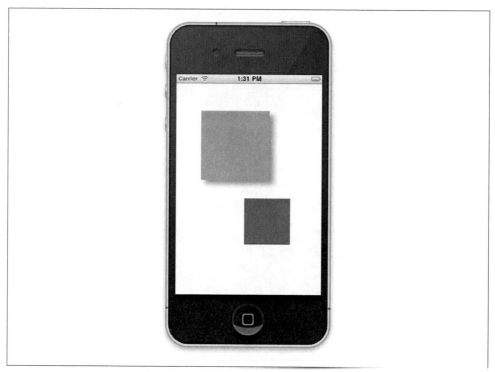

Figure 25. Saving the state of the graphics context for accurate shadows

Creating and Drawing Gradients

After learning about colors in "Constructing, Setting, and Using Colors" on page 13, we're ready to put our skills to better use than drawing simple rectangles and colorful text!

Core Graphics allows programmers to create two types of gradients: axial and radial. (We will only discuss axial gradients in this book.) Axial gradients are gradients that start from one point with one color and end at another point with another color (although they can start and stop with the same color, which does not make them much of a gradient). "Axial" means relating to an axis. The two points (start and end point) create a line segment, which will be the axis on which the gradient will be drawn. An example of an axial gradient is shown in Figure 26.

In order to create an axial gradient, you must call the CGGradientCreateWithColor Components function. The return value of this function will be the new gradient of type CGGradientRef. This is the handle to the gradient. Once you are done with the gradient, you *must* call the CGGradientRelease procedure, passing the handle to the gradient that you had previously retrieved from CGGradientCreateWithColorComponents.

Figure 26. An axial gradient, starting from the color blue and ending in the color green

The CGGradientCreateWithColorComponents function takes four parameters:

A color space
> This is a container for a range of colors, and must be of type CGColorSpaceRef. For this parameter, we can just pass the return value of the CGColorSpaceCreate DeviceRGB function, which will give us an RGB color space.

An array of color components (for details, see "Constructing, Setting, and Using Colors" on page 13)
> This array has to contain red, green, blue, and alpha values, all represented as CGFloat values. The number of elements in the array is tightly linked to the next two parameters. Essentially, you have to include enough values in this array to specify the number of locations in the fourth parameter. So if you ask for two locations (the start and end point), you have to provide two colors in the array here. And since each color is made out of red, green, blue, and alpha, this array has to have 2×4 items: four for the first color and four for the second. Don't worry if you didn't get all this, you will eventually understand it through the examples that follow in this section.

Locations of colors in the array of colors
> This parameter controls how quickly the gradient shifts from one color to another. The number of elements must be the same as the value of the fourth parameter. If

we ask for four colors, for example, and we want the first color to be the starting color and the last color to be the ending color in the gradient, we have to provide an array of two items of type CGFloats, with the first item set to 0.0f (as in the *first* item in the array of colors) and the second item set to 3.0f (as in the *fourth* item in the array of colors). The values of the two intermediate colors determine how the gradient actually inserts colors to get from the start to the end. Again, don't worry if this is too difficult to grasp. I will give you many examples to help you fully understand the concept.

Number of locations
This specifies how many colors and locations we want.

Let's have a look at an example. Suppose we want to draw the same gradient we saw in Figure 26? Here's how:

1. Pick the start and end points of the gradient—the axis along which it will shift. In this case, I've chosen to move from left to right. Think of this as changing color as you move along a hypothetical horizontal line. Along that line, we will spread the colors so that every perpendicular line to this horizontal line contains only one color. In this case, the perpendicular lines would be every vertical line in Figure 26. Look at those vertical lines closely. Every single one contains only one color, which runs all the way from top to the bottom. That's how axial gradients work. OK, that's enough theory—let's go to the second step.

2. Now we have to create a color space to pass to the first parameter of the CGGradientCreateWithColorComponents function, as mentioned before:

```
CGColorSpaceRef colorSpace =
  CGColorSpaceCreateDeviceRGB();
```

 We will release this color space once we are done with it.

3. Select blue as the starting point (left) and green as the ending point (right), according to the colors chosen in Figure 26. The names I've selected (startColorComponents and endColorComponents) are arbitrarily chosen to help us remember what we're doing with each color. We'll actually use array positions to specify which one is the start and which one is the end:

```
UIColor *startColor = [UIColor blueColor];
  CGFloat *startColorComponents =
  (CGFloat *)CGColorGetComponents([startColor CGColor]);

  UIColor *endColor = [UIColor greenColor];
  CGFloat *endColorComponents =
  (CGFloat *)CGColorGetComponents([endColor CGColor]);
```

If you don't remember the concept behind color components, I suggest that you look at the section "Constructing, Setting, and Using Colors" on page 13, before you continue reading these instructions.

4. After retrieving the components of each color, we place them all in one flat array to pass to the CGGradientCreateWithColorComponents function:

```
CGFloat colorComponents[8] = {

    /* Four components of the blue color (RGBA) */
    startColorComponents[0],
    startColorComponents[1],
    startColorComponents[2],
    startColorComponents[3], /* First color = blue */


    /* Four components of the green color (RGBA) */
    endColorComponents[0],
    endColorComponents[1],
    endColorComponents[2],
    endColorComponents[3], /* Second color = green */

};
```

5. Because we have only two colors in this array, we need to specify that the first is positioned at the very beginning of the gradient (position 0.0) and the second at the very end (position 1.0). So let's place these indices in an array to pass to the CGGradientCreateWithColorComponents function:

```
CGFloat colorIndices[2] = {
    0.0f, /* Color 0 in the colorComponents array */
    1.0f, /* Color 1 in the colorComponents array */
};
```

6. Now all we have to do is to actually call the CGGradientCreateWithColor Components function with all these values that we generated:

```
CGGradientRef gradient =
CGGradientCreateWithColorComponents
(colorSpace,
 (const CGFloat *)&colorComponents,
 (const CGFloat *)&colorIndices,
 2);
```

7. Fantastic! Now we have our gradient object in the gradient variable. Before we forget, we have to release the color space that we created using the CGColorSpace CreateDeviceRGB function:

```
CGColorSpaceRelease(colorSpace);
```

Now we'll use the `CGContextDrawLinearGradient` procedure to draw the axial gradient on a graphics context. This procedure takes five parameters:

Graphics context
> Specifies the graphics context on which the axial gradient will be drawn.

Axial gradient
> The handle to the axial gradient object. We created this gradient object using the `CGGradientCreateWithColorComponents` function.

Start point
> A point on the graphics context, specified by a `CGPoint`, that indicates the start point of the gradient.

End point
> A point on the graphics context, specified by a `CGPoint`, that indicates the end point of the gradient.

Gradient drawing options
> Specifies what happens if your start or end point isn't at the edge of the graphical context. You can use your start or end color to fill the space that lies outside the gradient. Specify one of the following values for this parameter:
>
> `kCGGradientDrawsAfterEndLocation`
> > Extends the gradient to all points after the ending point of the gradient.
>
> `kCGGradientDrawsBeforeStartLocation`
> > Extends the gradient to all points before the starting point of the gradient.
>
> `0`
> > Does not extend the gradient in any way.

To extend colors on both sides, specify both the "after" and "before" parameters as a logical OR (using the | operator). We'll see an example later:

```
CGRect screenBounds = [[UIScreen mainScreen] bounds];

CGPoint startPoint, endPoint;

startPoint = CGPointMake(0.0f,
                         screenBounds.size.height / 2.0f);

endPoint = CGPointMake(screenBounds.size.width,
                       startPoint.y);

CGContextDrawLinearGradient
(currentContext,
 gradient,
 startPoint,
 endPoint,
 0);

CGGradientRelease(gradient);
```

The gradient handle we are releasing at the end of this code was created in another code block in an earlier example.

The output of this code will obviously look similar to that shown in Figure 26. Because we started the gradient from the leftmost point of our view and stretched it all the way to the rightmost point, we couldn't take advantage of the values that could be passed to the final *Gradient drawing options* parameter of the CGContextDrawLinearGradient procedure. Let's remedy that, shall we? How about we draw a gradient that looks similar to that which is shown in Figure 27?

Figure 27. An axial gradient with start and end point color extensions

We will use the same procedure explained earlier in this section to code the result:

```
- (void)drawRect:(CGRect)rect{
// Drawing code

CGContextRef currentContext =
  UIGraphicsGetCurrentContext();

CGContextSaveGState(currentContext);
```

```
CGColorSpaceRef colorSpace =
  CGColorSpaceCreateDeviceRGB();

UIColor *startColor = [UIColor orangeColor];
CGFloat *startColorComponents =
  (CGFloat *)CGColorGetComponents([startColor CGColor]);

UIColor *endColor = [UIColor blueColor];
CGFloat *endColorComponents =
  (CGFloat *)CGColorGetComponents([endColor CGColor]);

CGFloat colorComponents[8] = {

  /* Four components of the orange color (RGBA) */
  startColorComponents[0],
  startColorComponents[1],
  startColorComponents[2],
  startColorComponents[3], /* First color = orange */


  /* Four components of the blue color (RGBA) */
  endColorComponents[0],
  endColorComponents[1],
  endColorComponents[2],
  endColorComponents[3], /* Second color = blue */

};

CGFloat colorIndices[2] = {
  0.0f, /* Color 0 in the colorComponents array */
  1.0f, /* Color 1 in the colorComponents array */
};

CGGradientRef gradient =
CGGradientCreateWithColorComponents
(colorSpace,
 (const CGFloat *)&colorComponents,
 (const CGFloat *)&colorIndices,
 2);

CGColorSpaceRelease(colorSpace);

CGPoint startPoint, endPoint;

startPoint = CGPointMake(120,
                         260);

endPoint = CGPointMake(200.0f,
                       220);

CGContextDrawLinearGradient
(currentContext,
 gradient,
 startPoint,
 endPoint,
```

```
        kCGGradientDrawsBeforeStartLocation |
        kCGGradientDrawsAfterEndLocation);

    CGGradientRelease(gradient);

    CGContextRestoreGState(currentContext);

}
```

It might be difficult to understand how mixing kCGGradientDrawsBeforeStartLocation and kCGGradientDrawsAfterEndLocation values passed to the CGContextDrawLinear Gradient procedure is creating a diagonal effect like that shown in Figure 27. So let's remove those values and set that parameter of the CGContextDrawLinearGradient procedure to 0 like we had it before. Figure 28 shows what the results will be.

Figure 28. Axial gradient without stretched colors

It's easy to conclude that the gradient in Figure 28 is the same gradient that we see in Figure 27. However, the gradient in Figure 27 extends the start and end points' colors all the way across the graphics context, which is why you can see the whole screen covered with color.

Displacing Shapes on Graphic Contexts

"Drawing Rectangles" on page 31 mentioned transformations. These are exactly what the name suggests: changes to the way a graphic is displayed. Transformations in Core Graphics are objects that you apply to shapes before they get drawn. For instance, you can create a translation transformation. Translating what, you might be asking? A translation transformation is a mechanism by which you can *displace* a shape or a graphics context.

Other types of transformations include rotation (see "Rotating Shapes Drawn on Graphic Contexts" on page 55) and scaling (see "Scaling Shapes Drawn on Graphic Contexts" on page 52). These are all examples of *affine* transformations, which map each point in the origin to another point in the final version. All the transformations we discuss in this book will be affine transformations.

A translation transformation *translates* the current position of a shape on a path or graphics context to another relative place. For instance, if you draw a point at location (10, 20), apply a translation transformation of (30, 40) to it, and then draw it, the point will be drawn at (40, 60), because 40 is the sum of 10+30 and 60 is the sum of 20+40.

In order to create a new translation transformation, we must use the `CGAffine TransformMakeTranslation` function, which will return an affine transformation of type `CGAffineTransform`. The two parameters to this function specify the *x* and the *y* translation in points.

In "Drawing Rectangles" on page 31, we saw that the `CGPathAddRect` procedure accepts, as its second parameter, a transformation object of type `CGAffineTransform`. To displace a rectangle from its original place to another, you can simply create an affine transformation specifying the changes you want to make in the *x* and *y* coordinates, and pass the transformation to the second parameter of the `CGPathAddRect` procedure as shown here:

```
- (void)drawRect:(CGRect)rect{
  // Drawing code

  /* Create the path first. Just the path handle. */
  CGMutablePathRef path = CGPathCreateMutable();

  /* Here are our rectangle boundaries */
  CGRect rectangle = CGRectMake(10.0f,
                                10.0f,
                                200.0f,
                                300.0f);

  /* We want to displace the rectangle to the right by
    100 points but want to keep the y position
    untouched */
  CGAffineTransform transform =
    CGAffineTransformMakeTranslation(100.0f,
                                     0.0f);
```

```
/* Add the rectangle to the path */
CGPathAddRect(path,
              &transform,
              rectangle);

/* Get the handle to the current context */
CGContextRef currentContext =
  UIGraphicsGetCurrentContext();

/* Add the path to the context */
CGContextAddPath(currentContext,
                 path);

/* Set the fill color to cornflower blue */
[[UIColor colorWithRed:0.20f
            green:0.60f
             blue:0.80f
            alpha:1.0f] setFill];

/* Set the stroke color to brown */
[[UIColor brownColor] setStroke];

/* Set the line width (for the stroke) to 5 */
CGContextSetLineWidth(currentContext,
                      5.0f);

/* Stroke and fill the path on the context */
CGContextDrawPath(currentContext,
                  kCGPathFillStroke);

/* Dispose of the path */
CGPathRelease(path);

}
```

Figure 29 shows the output of this block of code when placed inside a view object.

Compare Figure 29 with Figure 21. Can you see the difference? Check the source code for both figures and you'll see that the *x* and *y* points specified for both rectangles in both code blocks are the same. It is just that in Figure 29, we have applied an affine translation transformation to the rectangle when we added it to the path.

In addition to applying transformations to shapes that get drawn to a path, we can apply transformations to graphics contexts using the CGContextTranslateCTM procedure. This applies a translation transformation on the current transformation matrix (CTM). The current transformation matrix, although its name might be complex, is quite simple to understand. Think of CTM as how your graphics context's center is set up, and how each point that you draw gets projected onto the screen. For instance, when you ask Core Graphics to draw a point at (0, 0), Core Graphics finds the center of the screen by looking at the CTM. The CTM will then do some calculations and tell Core Graphics that point (0, 0) is indeed at the top-left corner of the screen. Using procedures such as CGContextTranslateCTM, you can change how CTM is configured

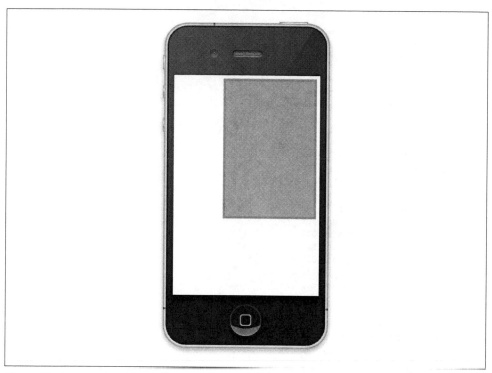

Figure 29. A rectangle with an affine translation transformation

and subsequently force every shape drawn on the graphics context to be shifted to another place on the canvas. Here is an example where we achieve the exact same effect we saw in Figure 29 by applying a translation transformation to the CTM instead of directly to our rectangle:

```
- (void)drawRect:(CGRect)rect{
  // Drawing code

  /* Create the path first. Just the path handle. */
  CGMutablePathRef path = CGPathCreateMutable();

  /* Here are our rectangle boundaries */
  CGRect rectangle = CGRectMake(10.0f,
                                10.0f,
                                200.0f,
                                300.0f);

  /* Add the rectangle to the path */
  CGPathAddRect(path,
                NULL,
                rectangle);

  /* Get the handle to the current context */
  CGContextRef currentContext =
    UIGraphicsGetCurrentContext();
```

```
/* Save the state of the context to revert
 back to how it was at this state, later */
CGContextSaveGState(currentContext);

/* Translate the current transformation matrix
 to the right by 100 points */
CGContextTranslateCTM(currentContext,
                      100.0f,
                      0.0f);

/* Add the path to the context */
CGContextAddPath(currentContext,
                 path);

/* Set the fill color to cornflower blue */
[[UIColor colorWithRed:0.20f
                 green:0.60f
                  blue:0.80f
                 alpha:1.0f] setFill];

/* Set the stroke color to brown */
[[UIColor brownColor] setStroke];

/* Set the line width (for the stroke) to 5 */
CGContextSetLineWidth(currentContext,
                      5.0f);

/* Stroke and fill the path on the context */
CGContextDrawPath(currentContext,
                  kCGPathFillStroke);

/* Dispose of the path */
CGPathRelease(path);

/* Restore the state of the context */
CGContextRestoreGState(currentContext);

}
```

After running this program, you will notice that the results are exactly like those shown in Figure 29.

Scaling Shapes Drawn on Graphic Contexts

"Displacing Shapes on Graphic Contexts" on page 49 explained what a transformation is, and how to apply it to shapes and graphics contexts. One of the transformations that you can apply is scaling. You can easily ask Core Graphics to scale a shape, such as a circle, to 100 times its original size.

To create an affine scale transformation, use the CGAffineTransformMakeScale function, which returns a transformation object of type CGAffineTransform. If you want to apply a scale transformation directly to a graphics context, use the `CGContextScaleCTM` procedure to scale the Current Transformation Matrix (CTM). For more information about CTM, see "Displacing Shapes on Graphic Contexts" on page 49.

Scale transformation functions take two parameters: one to scale the *x* axis and the other to scale the *y* axis. Take another look at the rectangle in Figure 21. If we want to scale this rectangle to half its normal length and width, shown in Figure 21, we can simply scale the *x* and the *y* axis by 0.5 (half their original value), as shown here:

```
/* Scale the rectangle to half its size */
CGAffineTransform transform =
  CGAffineTransformMakeScale(0.5f, 0.5f);

/* Add the rectangle to the path */
CGPathAddRect(path,
              &transform,
              rectangle);
```

Figure 30 shows what we will see after applying the scale transformation to the code we wrote in "Drawing Rectangles" on page 31.

Figure 30. Scaling a rectangle

In addition to the `CGAffineTransformMakeScale` function, you can use the `CGContext ScaleCTM` procedure to apply a scale transformation to a graphics context. The following code will achieve the exact same effect as the previous example, as you can see in Figure 30:

```objc
- (void)drawRect:(CGRect)rect{
// Drawing code

/* Create the path first. Just the path handle. */
CGMutablePathRef path = CGPathCreateMutable();

/* Here are our rectangle boundaries */
CGRect rectangle = CGRectMake(10.0f,
                              10.0f,
                              200.0f,
                              300.0f);

/* Add the rectangle to the path */
CGPathAddRect(path,
              NULL,
              rectangle);

/* Get the handle to the current context */
CGContextRef currentContext =
  UIGraphicsGetCurrentContext();

/* Scale everything drawn on the current
 graphics context to half its size */
CGContextScaleCTM(currentContext,
                  0.5f,
                  0.5f);

/* Add the path to the context */
CGContextAddPath(currentContext,
                 path);

/* Set the fill color to cornflower blue */
[[UIColor colorWithRed:0.20f
                green:0.60f
                 blue:0.80f
                alpha:1.0f] setFill];

/* Set the stroke color to brown */
[[UIColor brownColor] setStroke];

/* Set the line width (for the stroke) to 5 */
CGContextSetLineWidth(currentContext,
                      5.0f);

/* Stroke and fill the path on the context */
CGContextDrawPath(currentContext,
                  kCGPathFillStroke);

/* Dispose of the path */
CGPathRelease(path);

}
```

Rotating Shapes Drawn on Graphic Contexts

 I strongly suggest that you read the material in "Displacing Shapes on Graphic Contexts" on page 49 and in "Scaling Shapes Drawn on Graphic Contexts" on page 52 before proceeding with this section. To avoid redundancy of material, I have tried to keep material that has been taught in earlier sections out of later sections.

Just like scaling and translation, you can apply rotation translation to shapes drawn on paths, and graphics contexts. You can use the `CGAffineTransformMakeRotation` function and pass the rotation value in radians to get back a rotation transformation, of type `CGAffineTransform`. You can then apply this transformation to paths and shapes. If you want to rotate the whole context by a specific angle, you must use the `CGContext RotateCTM` procedure.

Let's rotate the same rectangle we had in Figure 21 45 degrees clockwise (see Figure 31). The values you supply for rotation must be in radians. Positive values cause clockwise rotation, while negative values cause counterclockwise rotation:

```
/* Rotate the rectangle 45 degrees clockwise */
CGAffineTransform transform =
  CGAffineTransformMakeRotation((45.0f * M_PI) / 180.0f);

/* Add the rectangle to the path */
CGPathAddRect(path,
              &transform,
              rectangle);
```

As we saw in "Scaling Shapes Drawn on Graphic Contexts" on page 52, we can also apply a transformation directly to a graphics context using the `CGContext RotateCTM` procedure.

Animating and Moving Views

There are various ways of performing animations in iOS: capabilities are provided at a relatively low level, but also at a higher level. The highest level we can get is through UIKit, which is what we will be discussing in this section. UIKit includes some low-level Core Animation functionalities and presents us with a really clean API to work with.

The starting point for performing animations in UIKit is to call the `beginAnimations:context:` class method of the `UIView` class. Its first parameter is an optional name that you choose for your animation, and the second is an optional context that you can retrieve later to pass to delegate methods of the animations. We will talk about these shortly.

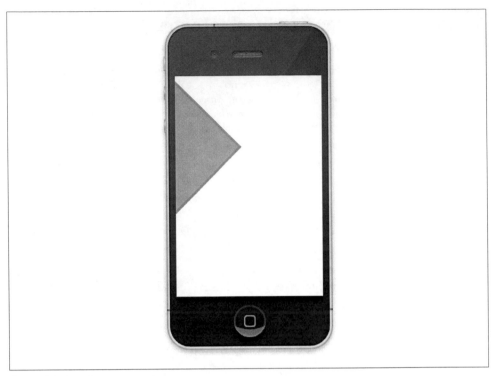

Figure 31. Rotating a rectangle

After you start an animation with the `beginAnimations:context:` method, it won't actually take place until you call the `commitAnimations` class method of `UIView` class. The calculation you perform on a view object (such as moving it) between calling `beginAni``mations:context:` and `commitAnimations` will be animated after the `commitAnimations` call. Let's have a look at an example.

As we saw in "Drawing Images" on page 18, I included in my bundle an image called *Xcode.png*. This is Xcode's icon, which I found by searching in Google Images (see Figure 14). Now, in my view controller (see "Creating the Project Structure in Xcode" on page 3), I want to place this image in an image view of type `UIImageView` and then move that image view from the top-left corner of the screen to the bottom-right corner.

 Discussing image views and their different properties is out of this book's scope. For more information, please refer to the *iOS 4 Programming Cookbook* (*http://oreilly.com/catalog/0636920010180*) (O'Reilly).

Here are the steps that complete this task:

1. Open the *.h* file of your view controller. If you followed the instructions in "Creating the Project Structure in Xcode" on page 3, this file will be named *GraphicsViewController.h* in your project.

2. Define an instance of `UIImageView` as a property of the view controller, and call it `xcodeImageView`, like so:

```
#import <UIKit/UIKit.h>

@interface GraphicsViewController : UIViewController {
@protected
  UIImageView *xcodeImageView;
}

@property (nonatomic, retain) UIImageView *xcodeImageView;

@end
```

3. In the *.m* file of your view controller, *GraphicsViewController.m*, synthesize the image view you created in the previous step and make sure you dispose of it when the time comes:

```
#import "GraphicsViewController.h"

@implementation GraphicsViewController

@synthesize xcodeImageView;

- (void)dealloc{
  [super dealloc];
}

- (void)viewDidUnload{
  [super viewDidUnload];
  self.xcodeImageView = nil;
}

@end
```

4. Load the *Xcode.png* image into an instance of `UIImage` during the initialization of your view controller, like so:

```
- (id) initWithNibName:(NSString *)nibNameOrNil
               bundle:(NSBundle *)nibBundleOrNil{

  self = [super initWithNibName:nibNameOrNil
                       bundle:nibBundleOrNil];

  if (self != nil){

    UIImage *xcodeImage = [UIImage imageNamed:@"Xcode.png"];

    xcodeImageView = [[UIImageView alloc]
                     initWithImage:xcodeImage];
```

```
                    /* Just set the size to make the image smaller */
                    [xcodeImageView setFrame:CGRectMake(0.0f,
                                                        0.0f,
                                                        100.0f,
                                                        100.0f)];

        }
    return self;
}
```

5. When your view controller's view is loaded, in the `viewDidLoad` instance method, add your image view to your view controller's view in order for it to become visible to the user:

```
- (void) viewDidLoad{
    [super viewDidLoad];

    UIImage *xcodeImage = [UIImage imageNamed:@"Xcode.png"];

    xcodeImageView = [[UIImageView alloc]
                        initWithImage:xcodeImage];

    /* Just set the size to make the image smaller */
    [xcodeImageView setFrame:CGRectMake(0.0f,
                                        0.0f,
                                        100.0f,
                                        100.0f)];

    self.view.backgroundColor = [UIColor whiteColor];
    [self.view addSubview:self.xcodeImageView];

}
```

6. Figure 32 shows how our view will look when we run our program in iOS Simulator.

7. Now when our view appears on the screen, in the `viewDidAppear:` instance method of our view controller, we will start the animation block for our image view and start an animation that moves the image from its initial location at the top-left corner of the screen to the bottom-right corner. We will make sure this animation happens over a 5-second time period:

```
- (void) viewDidAppear:(BOOL)paramAnimated{

    [super viewDidAppear:paramAnimated];

    /* Start from top left corner */
    [self.xcodeImageView setFrame:CGRectMake(0.0f,
                                             0.0f,
                                             100.0f,
                                             100.0f)];

    [UIView beginAnimations:@"xcodeImageViewAnimation"
                    context:xcodeImageView];
```

Figure 32. Adding an image view to a view object

```
    /* 5 seconds animation */
    [UIView setAnimationDuration:5.0f];

    /* Receive animation delegates */
    [UIView setAnimationDelegate:self];

    [UIView setAnimationDidStopSelector:
     @selector(imageViewDidStop:finished:context:)];

    /* End at the bottom right corner */
    [self.xcodeImageView setFrame:CGRectMake(200.0f,
                                             350.0f,
                                             100.0f,
                                             100.0f)];

    [UIView commitAnimations];

}
```

8. Provide the implementation for a `imageViewDidStop:finished:context:` delegate method for your view controller so that it gets called by UIKit when the animation finishes. This is optional, and for our example I will just log some messages to prove that the method was called. Later examples will show how you can use the method to kick off other activity the moment the animation is finished:

```
- (void)imageViewDidStop:(NSString *)paramAnimationID
                finished:(NSNumber *)paramFinished
                 context:(void *)paramContext{
    NSLog(@"Animation finished.");

    NSLog(@"Animation ID = %@", paramAnimationID);

    UIImageView *contextImageView = (UIImageView *)paramContext;
    NSLog(@"Image View = %@", contextImageView);

}
```

Now if you run the app, you will notice that as soon as your view gets displayed, the image shown in Figure 32 will start moving towards the bottom-right corner, as shown in Figure 33, over a period of 5 seconds.

Figure 33. The image is animated to the bottom-right corner of the screen

Also, if you look at the output printed to the console, you will see something similar to this if you wait for the animation to finish:

```
Animation finished.
Animation ID = xcodeImageViewAnimation
Image View = <UIImageView: 0x4e2b180; frame = (200 350; 100 100);
  opaque = NO; userInteractionEnabled = NO;
  layer = <CALayer: 0x4e2b1b0>>
```

Now let's go through some of the concepts and how we actually animated this image view. Here are the important class methods of `UIView` that you should know about when performing animations using UIKit:

`beginAnimations:context:`
> Starts an animation block. Any animatable property change that you apply to views after calling this class method will be animated after the animation is committed.

`setAnimationDuration:`
> Sets the duration of the animation in seconds.

`setAnimationDelegate:`
> Sets the object that will receive delegate objects for various events that could happen before, during, or after the animation. Setting a delegate object will *not* immediately start firing animation delegates. You must also use different setter class methods on the view object to tell UIKit which selectors in your delegate object have to receive which delegate messages.

`setAnimationDidStopSelector:`
> Sets the method in the delegate object that has to be called when the animation finishes. This method has to accept three parameters in this order:
> 1. An animation identifier of type `NSString`: this will contain the animation identifier passed to the `beginAnimations:context:` class method of `UIView` when the animation was started.
> 2. A "finished" indicator, of type `NSNumber`: this parameter contains a boolean value inside the `NSNumber`, which the run-time sets to YES if it could fully finish the animation before it was stopped by the code. If this is value is set to NO, it means the animation was interrupted before it was completed.
> 3. A context of type `void *`: this is the context that was passed to the `beginAnimations:context:` class method of `UIView` when the animation was started.

`setAnimationWillStartSelector:`
> Sets the selector that has to be called in the delegate object when the animation is about to start. The selector passed to this class method has to have two parameters, in this order:
> 1. An animation identifier of type `NSString`: the runtime sets this to the animation identifier passed to the `beginAnimations:context:` class method of `UIView` when the animation was started.
> 2. A context of type `void *`: this is the context that was passed to the `beginAnimations:context:` class method of `UIView` when the animation was started.

`setAnimationDelay:`
> Sets a delay (in seconds) for the animation before it starts. If this value is set to `3.0f`, for instance, the animation will start 3 seconds after it has been committed.

`setAnimationRepeatCount:`
> Sets the number of times an animation block has to repeat its animation.

Now that we know some of the most useful `UIView` class methods that help us animate views, let's look at another animation. In this example code, I want to have two image views, both displaying the same image, to appear on the screen at the same time: one at the top-left corner and the other at the bottom-right corner, as shown in Figure 34.

Figure 34. The starting position of the animation

 In this section, I will call the top-left image *image 1* and the bottom-right image *image 2*.

What we are going to do in this code is create two images, as mentioned, in the top-left and bottom-right corners. Next, we want *image 1* to start moving towards *image 2* over a 3-second period, and then fade away. While *image 1* is approaching *image 2*, we want *image 2* to start its animation and move towards the top-left corner of the screen, where *image 1* used to be. We also want *image 2* to complete its animation over a 3-second time period, and fade away at the end. This will look *really* cool when you run it on a device or the iOS Simulator. Let me show you how to code it:

1. In the *.h* file of your view controller, define two image views:

```
@interface GraphicsViewController : UIViewController {
@protected
  UIImageView *xcodeImageView1;
  UIImageView *xcodeImageView2;
}

@property (nonatomic, retain) UIImageView *xcodeImageView1;
@property (nonatomic, retain) UIImageView *xcodeImageView2;

@end
```

2. In the *.m* file of the view controller, make sure that you synthesize these two image views, because they are properties. Properties are explained thoroughly in the *iOS 4 Programming Cookbook* (*http://oreilly.com/catalog/0636920010180*) (O'Reilly):

```
#import "GraphicsViewController.h"

@implementation GraphicsViewController

@synthesize xcodeImageView1;
@synthesize xcodeImageView2;


... rest of the code
```

3. Make sure you deallocate both image views when the view is unloaded or deallocated:

```
- (void)dealloc{
  [xcodeImageView1 release];
  [xcodeImageView2 release];
  [super dealloc];
}

- (void)viewDidUnload{
  [super viewDidUnload];
  self.xcodeImageView1 = nil;
  self.xcodeImageView2 = nil;
}
```

4. In the `viewDidLoad` instance method of your view controller, initialize both of the image views and place them on your view:

```
- (void) viewDidLoad{
  [super viewDidLoad];

  UIImage *xcodeImage = [UIImage imageNamed:@"Xcode.png"];

  xcodeImageView1 = [[UIImageView alloc]
                    initWithImage:xcodeImage];

  xcodeImageView2 = [[UIImageView alloc]
                    initWithImage:xcodeImage];
```

```
/* Just set the size to make the images smaller */
[xcodeImageView1 setFrame:CGRectMake(0.0f,
                                     0.0f,
                                     100.0f,
                                     100.0f)];

[xcodeImageView2 setFrame:CGRectMake(220.0f,
                                     350.0f,
                                     100.0f,
                                     100.0f)];


self.view.backgroundColor = [UIColor whiteColor];
[self.view addSubview:self.xcodeImageView1];
[self.view addSubview:self.xcodeImageView2];

}
```

5. Implement an instance method called startTopLeftImageViewAnimation for your view controller. This method, as its name suggests, will carry out the animation for *image 1*, moving it from the top-left corner of the screen to the bottom-right corner while fading it out. Fading is accomplished simply by setting the alpha value to 0:

```
- (void) startTopLeftImageViewAnimation{

/* Start from top left corner */
[self.xcodeImageView1 setFrame:CGRectMake(0.0f,
                                          0.0f,
                                          100.0f,
                                          100.0f)];

[self.xcodeImageView1 setAlpha:1.0f];

[UIView beginAnimations:@"xcodeImageView1Animation"
                context:xcodeImageView1];

/* 3 seconds animation */
[UIView setAnimationDuration:3.0f];

/* Receive animation delegates */
[UIView setAnimationDelegate:self];

[UIView setAnimationDidStopSelector:
 @selector(imageViewDidStop:finished:context:)];

/* End at the bottom right corner */
[self.xcodeImageView1 setFrame:CGRectMake(220.0f,
                                          350.0f,
                                          100.0f,
                                          100.0f)];

[self.xcodeImageView1 setAlpha:0.0f];
```

```
[UIView commitAnimations];

}
```

6. When the animation for any of these image views stops, we intend to remove those image views from their parent views, as they are not useful anymore. As we saw in the `startTopLeftImageViewAnimation` method, we passed a delegate selector to the `setAnimationDidStopSelector:` class method of `UIView`, and this selector will get called when the animations for *image 1* (as we saw before) and for *image 2* (as we will soon see) stop. Here is the implementation for this delegate selector:

```
- (void)imageViewDidStop:(NSString *)paramAnimationID
                finished:(NSNumber *)paramFinished
                 context:(void *)paramContext{

    UIImageView *contextImageView = (UIImageView *)paramContext;
    [contextImageView removeFromSuperview];

}
```

7. We also need a method that will animate *image 2*. There is a little difference between how I've written the animation method for *image 2* as compared to that for *image 1*. I want to be able to start *image 2*'s animation *almost* as *image 1* is finishing its animation. So if *image 1* performs its animation in 3 seconds, I want *image 2* to start its animation at second 2.0 in *image 1*'s animation, so that I can see *image 2* starting to animate before *image 1* gets to the bottom right of the screen and fades away. To accomplish this, I am starting both animations at the same time, but the animation for *image 2* will include a 2-second delay at the beginning. So if I start both animations at 1 p.m., *image 1* will start its animation at 13:00:00 and finish it at 13:00:03, while *image 2* starts at 13:00:02 and finishes at 13:00:05. Here is how we will animate *image 2*:

```
- (void) startBottomRightViewAnimationAfterDelay:
(CGFloat)paramDelay{

    /* Start from bottom right corner */
    [self.xcodeImageView2 setFrame:CGRectMake(220.0f,
                                              350.0f,
                                              100.0f,
                                              100.0f)];

    [self.xcodeImageView2 setAlpha:1.0f];

    [UIView beginAnimations:@"xcodeImageView2Animation"
                    context:xcodeImageView2];

    /* 3 seconds animation */
    [UIView setAnimationDuration:3.0f];

    [UIView setAnimationDelay:paramDelay];
```

```
/* Receive animation delegates */
[UIView setAnimationDelegate:self];

[UIView setAnimationDidStopSelector:
 @selector(imageViewDidStop:finished:context:)];

/* End at the top left corner */
[self.xcodeImageView2 setFrame:CGRectMake(0.0f,
                                          0.0f,
                                          100.0f,
                                          100.0f)];

[self.xcodeImageView2 setAlpha:0.0f];

[UIView commitAnimations];

}
```

8. Last but not least, we have to fire both the `startTopLeftImageViewAnimation` and the `startBottomRightViewAnimationAfterDelay:` methods at the same time when our view becomes visible:

```
- (void) viewDidAppear:(BOOL)paramAnimated{

[super viewDidAppear:paramAnimated];
[self startTopLeftImageViewAnimation];
[self startBottomRightViewAnimationAfterDelay:2.0f];

}
```

Animating and Scaling Views

 I highly recommend that you read "Animating and Moving Views" on page 55 before proceeding with this section of the book.

In order to scale a view while animating it, you can either apply a scale transformation to it within an animation block (see "Scaling Shapes Drawn on Graphic Contexts" on page 52), or just increase the view's width and/or height.

Let's have a look at scaling an image view by applying a scale transformation to it:

```
- (void) viewDidAppear:(BOOL)paramAnimated{

[super viewDidAppear:paramAnimated];

/* Place the image view at the center of the
 view of this view controller */
self.xcodeImageView.center = self.view.center;
```

```
/* Make sure no translation is applied to this image view */
self.xcodeImageView.transform = CGAffineTransformIdentity;

/* Begin the animation */
[UIView beginAnimations:nil
               context:NULL];

/* Make the animation 5 seconds long */
[UIView setAnimationDuration:5.0f];

/* Make the image view twice as large in
   width and height */
self.xcodeImageView.transform =
  CGAffineTransformMakeScale(2.0f,
                             2.0f);

/* Commit the animation */
[UIView commitAnimations];

}
```

This code uses an affine scale transformation to scale the image view to become twice as big as it originally was. The best thing about applying scale transformations to a view is that the width and height are scaled using the center of the view as the center of the scaling. Suppose that the center of your view is at point (100, 100) on the screen, and you scale your view to be twice as big in width and height. The resulting view will have its center remain at point (100, 100) on the screen, while being twice as big in each direction. If you were to scale a view by increasing its frame's width and height explicitly, you would end up with the final view being located somewhere else on the screen. That's because when changing the frame of the image view to scale the width and height, you are also changing the value of the *x* and the *y* of the frame, whether you want to or not. Because of that, your image view will not be scaled up from its center. Fixing this issue is outside the scope of this book, but feel free to play with it for a while and maybe you will find the solution. One hint that I *will* give you is that you can run two animations at the same time in parallel: one for changing the width and height, and the other for changing the center of the image view!

Animating and Rotating Views

 I highly recommend that you read "Animating and Moving Views" on page 55 before proceeding with this section of the book.

In order to rotate a view while animating it, you must apply a rotation transformation to it while in an animation block (see "Scaling Shapes Drawn on Graphic Contexts" on page 52). Let's have a look at some sample code which will make this clearer.

Let's say we have an image named *Xcode.png* (see Figure 14), and we want to display it in the center of the screen. After the image is displayed, we want to rotate it 90 degrees over a 5-second time period and then rotate it back to its original orientation. So when our view appears on the screen, let's rotate the image view 90 degrees clockwise:

```
- (void) viewDidAppear:(BOOL)paramAnimated{
  [super viewDidAppear:paramAnimated];

  self.xcodeImageView.center = self.view.center;

  /* Begin the animation */
  [UIView beginAnimations:@"clockwiseAnimation"
                  context:NULL];

  /* Make the animation 5 seconds long */
  [UIView setAnimationDuration:5.0f];

  [UIView setAnimationDelegate:self];

  [UIView setAnimationDidStopSelector:
   @selector(clockwiseRotationStopped:finished:context:)];

  /* Rotate the image view 90 degrees */
  self.xcodeImageView.transform =
  CGAffineTransformMakeRotation((90.0f * M_PI) / 180.0f);

  /* Commit the animation */
  [UIView commitAnimations];

}
```

We've chosen the clockwiseRotationStopped:finished:context: selector to get called when the clockwise rotation animation finishes. In that method, we will be rotating the image view counterclockwise back to 0 degrees (where it originally was) over a 5-second time period:

```
- (void)clockwiseRotationStopped:(NSString *)paramAnimationID
                        finished:(NSNumber *)paramFinished
                         context:(void *)paramContext{

  [UIView beginAnimations:@"counterclockwiseAnimation"
                  context:NULL];

  /* 5 seconds long */
  [UIView setAnimationDuration:5.0f];

  /* Back to original rotation */
  self.xcodeImageView.transform =
  CGAffineTransformIdentity;

  [UIView commitAnimations];

}
```

As you saw in "Animating and Moving Views" on page 55, "Animating and Scaling Views" on page 66, and in this section, there are many ways to animate views (direct or indirect subclasses of UIView) and many properties that you can modify while carrying out your animations. Be creative and inspect other properties in UIView which you might have not previously known about. You may also want to take a look at the documentation for UIView in Xcode Organizer.

The information you need, when and where you need it.

With Safari Books Online, you can:

Access the contents of thousands of technology and business books

- Quickly search over 7000 books and certification guides
- Download whole books or chapters in PDF format, at no extra cost, to print or read on the go
- Copy and paste code
- Save up to 35% on O'Reilly print books
- **New!** Access mobile-friendly books directly from cell phones and mobile devices

Stay up-to-date on emerging topics before the books are published

- Get on-demand access to evolving manuscripts.
- Interact directly with authors of upcoming books

Explore thousands of hours of video on technology and design topics

- Learn from expert video tutorials
- Watch and replay recorded conference sessions

O'REILLY®

Spreading the knowledge of innovators   safari.oreilly.com

Get even more for your money.

Join the O'Reilly Community, and register the O'Reilly books you own. It's free, and you'll get:

- $4.99 ebook upgrade offer
- 40% upgrade offer on O'Reilly print books
- Membership discounts on books and events
- Free lifetime updates to ebooks and videos
- Multiple ebook formats, DRM FREE
- Participation in the O'Reilly community
- Newsletters
- Account management
- 100% Satisfaction Guarantee

Signing up is easy:

1. **Go to: oreilly.com/go/register**
2. **Create an O'Reilly login.**
3. **Provide your address.**
4. **Register your books.**

Note: English-language books only

To order books online:
oreilly.com/store

For questions about products or an order:
orders@oreilly.com

To sign up to get topic-specific email announcements and/or news about upcoming books, conferences, special offers, and new technologies:
elists@oreilly.com

For technical questions about book content:
booktech@oreilly.com

To submit new book proposals to our editors:
proposals@oreilly.com

O'Reilly books are available in multiple DRM-free ebook formats. For more information:
oreilly.com/ebooks

O'REILLY®

Spreading the knowledge of innovators   oreilly.com

CPSIA information can be obtained at www.ICGtesting.com
Printed in the USA
239588LV00003B/11/P

9 781449 305673